# Stars

### illustrated by

## Rhoda and Robert Burns

## Starters Facts · Green 4
### Macdonald Educational

At night we can see the stars. They shine
in the dark sky. During the day, the sky
is too bright for us to see the stars.
On a clear night, though, we can see
hundreds. But there are many more stars
which are so faint we can only just see
them, and others that are so far away
we can't see them at all.

The sun is a star, and it is the nearest star to us. It is 150 million kilometres from the Earth. The other stars are much, much further away, which is why they look like tiny points of light. Some time in the future, people may travel to the stars in spaceships.

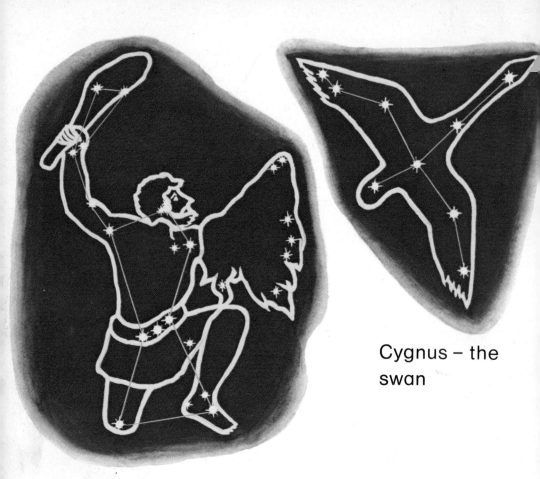

Cygnus – the
swan

Orion – the
hunter

Long ago, people who looked at the
stars saw that they always stayed in
the same patterns. These patterns were
called constellations. They were all
given names.

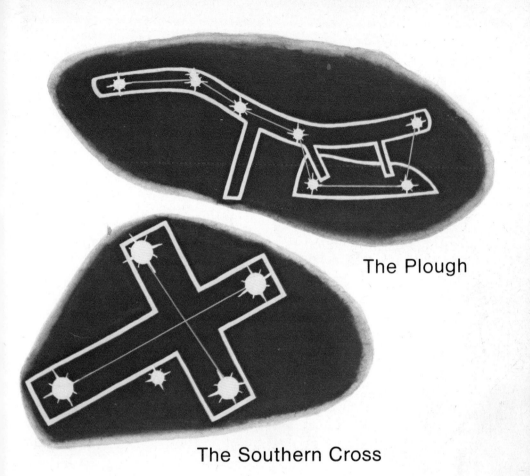

The Plough

The Southern Cross

Because the Earth goes round, the constellations seem to move through the sky at night. You can see different constellations from different parts of the world. In northern countries you can see the Plough. In southern countries you can see the Southern Cross.

The Milky Way

The Sun belongs to a group of millions of
stars. This group is called the Galaxy.
The part of the Galaxy that we can see is
called the Milky Way. There are many
other galaxies in space, which are much
further away. The whole of space is
called the Universe.

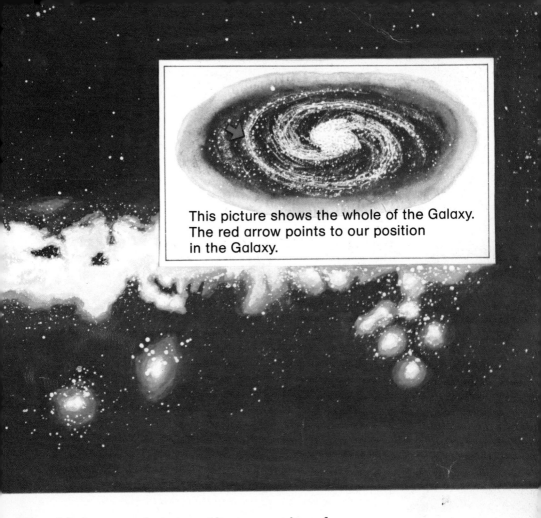

This picture shows the whole of the Galaxy.
The red arrow points to our position
in the Galaxy.

The Universe began thousands of
millions of years ago. Some people say
that there was a big bang and the
galaxies formed. The galaxies moved
away from each other, and out into
space. The Universe is still getting
bigger and bigger.

Stars do not last forever. They are born,
and they die millions of years later. Stars
are made of a gas called hydrogen. The
picture shows a cloud of gas, in which
new stars are being made.

1. The Sun began as a cloud of gas floating in space.

2. **The middle of the cloud got very hot.**

3. It became the Sun. The Sun will shine for millions of years.

4. Then the gas at its centre will run out, and the Sun will get smaller.

5. Before the Sun dies, it will swell up again.

8. The Sun will die, and will become a cold, dark object in space.

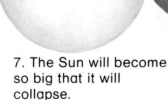

7. The Sun will become so big that it will collapse.

6 It will get much bigger and become a giant red star. The Earth will be burned up.

The Sun is an ordinary star. It looks different to other stars because it is so much nearer to us. It will not die for millions of years. Some stars are much bigger and hotter than the Sun. They would burn up the Earth if they were as near as the Sun.

Many stars form in pairs called double
stars. Double stars always stay together.
There are also groups of stars called star
clusters. There is a star cluster in this
picture.

10

An exploding star

Very big stars explode when they die. They become so bright that you can see them during the day. After the explosion, a black hole may be left behind. It is not really a hole, but a small star that sucks in everything around it.

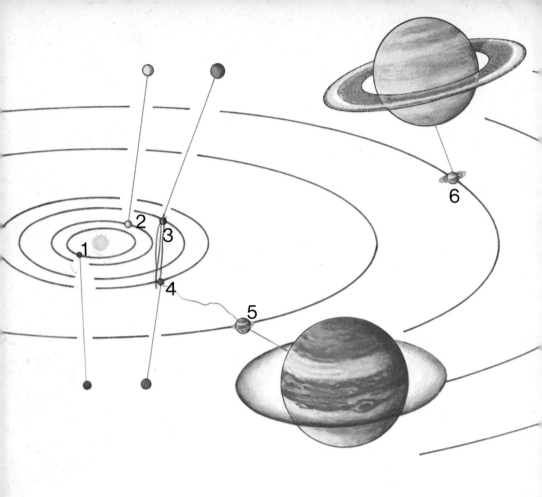

The Earth is a planet. Planets are
different from stars. Stars are hot, and
give out light and heat. Planets are cold.
They are lit up by the light from a star.
The Earth is lit by the Sun.

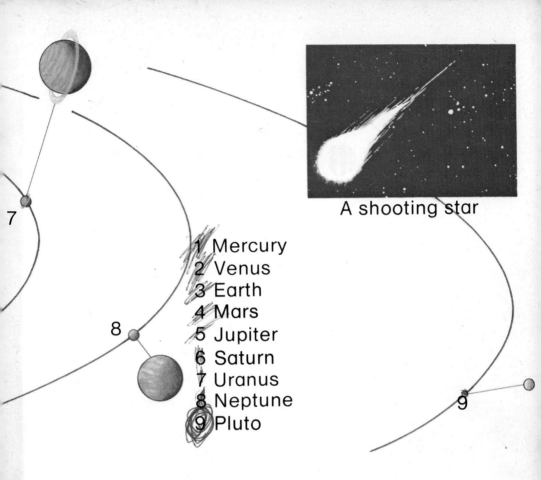

A shooting star

1 Mercury
2 Venus
3 Earth
4 Mars
5 Jupiter
6 Saturn
7 Uranus
8 Neptune
9 Pluto

The Earth is not the only planet. Eight
more planets go round the Sun. Far
away in space there may be planets
going round other stars.
Sometimes you may see 'shooting stars'
high in the sky. These are not real stars,
but pieces of rock burning in the sky.

day time

night time

Light and heat come through space to us from our star, the Sun. We get day time and night time because the world goes round. During the day we face the Sun. It is light and may be warm. At night we are turned away from the Sun, and it is dark and cold.

In the summer, the Sun often gives us so
much light and heat that we can lie on
the beach and swim in the sea. Without
the Sun it would be so cold and dark that
we would die.

Without the Sun, plants would not be able to grow. We live by eating plants, or by eating animals that eat plants.
Without the Sun, we would not have any food. The Sun's light and heat also helps to make wood, coal and oil which we need for heat and energy.

It is hot in the summer and cold in the
winter. This is because the Sun is high in
the sky in the summer, and low in the sky
in the winter. In some places the Sun is
always high in the sky, so it is always hot.
We call these places tropical.

As the Earth goes round, the Sun seems
to move through the sky during the day.
You can tell the time by seeing where the
Sun is in the sky. Do you know how a
sundial works?

Once a year on June 21st, which is
Midsummer's Day, the Sun rises over the
huge stones at Stonehenge.
Stonehenge is an ancient temple in the
south of England, built nearly 4000
years ago. It may have been used to
work out how the Sun moves through the sky.

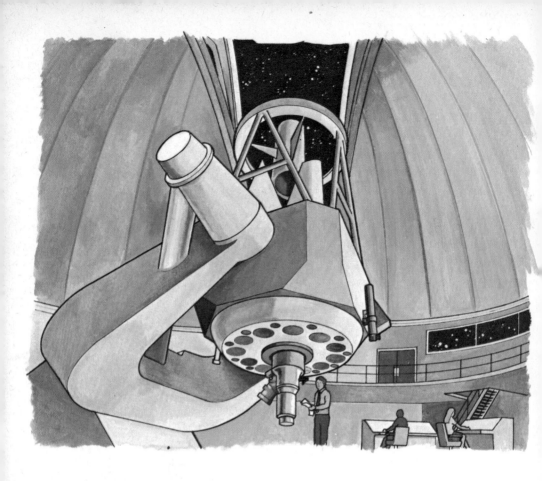

People who find out about stars are
called astronomers. They work in places
called observatories. Astronomers look
at stars through telescopes. A telescope
makes the stars look much brighter. It
helps the astronomer find faint stars in
the sky.

Stars send out radio waves as well as
light rays. Astronomers use radio
telescopes to pick up these radio waves.
They can find out about stars which are
far away in space, and cannot be seen
with ordinary telescopes.

Sailors use the Sun and stars to find out
the position of their ships at sea. They
use a sextant to show them how high the
Sun or stars are in the sky. The sextant
helps them to work out where they are.

The sailor is looking at a map of the sea.
The Sun and the stars help to show him
exactly where the ship is. He draws lines
on his map — where they cross is the
place where the ship is.

# Stars Activity

As the Sun moves through the sky, it casts shadows on the ground. Get up early on a sunny day, and try making your own sundial — it is very easy!

1. Find a sturdy stick. Make a hole for it in a patch of open ground.

2. The stick will cast a shadow on the ground.

3. Mark the end of the shadow every hour, on the hour.

4. Check the time with a watch, or a clock.

5. Paint the hours on the stones. If the sun goes in, come back another day and fill in the missing hours.

# Stars Quiz

These two constellations make pictures in the sky. Trace them out on to paper. Join up the dots. Try and find out their names.

# Stars Puzzle

The sailing ship is lost! The Captain does not know which way to go. Can you help him? Which star map should he look at?

# Stars Word List

| | | | |
|---|---|---|---|
| constellation page 4 |  | sundial page 18 |  |
| galaxy page 6 |  | temple page 19 |  |
| star cluster page 10 |  | astronomer page 20 |  |
| planet page 12 |  | radio telescope page 21 |  |
| shooting star page 13 |  | sextant page 22 |  |